MARDI GRAS

BY ANN HEINRICHS · ILLUSTRATED BY JAN BRYAN-HUNT

Published in the United States of America by The Child's World®
PO Box 326 • Chanhassen, MN 55317-0326
800-599-READ • www.childsworld.com

ACKNOWLEDGMENTS
The Child's World®: Mary Berendes, Publishing Director

Editorial Directions, Inc.: E. Russell Primm, Editorial Director; Katie Marsico, Managing Editor; Judith Shiffer, Assistant Editor; Caroline Wood and Rory Mabin, Editorial Assistants; Susan Hindman, Copy Editor and Proofreader; Elizabeth Nellums, Rory Mabin, Ruth Martin, and Caroline Wood, Fact Checkers; Tim Griffin/ IndexServ, Indexer

The Design Lab: Kathleen Petelinsek, Design and Page Production

LIBRARY OF CONGRESS CATALOGING-IN-PUBLICATION DATA
Heinrichs, Ann.
  Mardi Gras / by Ann Heinrichs ; illustrated by Jan Bryan-Hunt.
    p. cm. — (Holidays, festivals, & celebrations)
  Includes index.
  ISBN 1-59296-578-4 (library bound : alk. paper)
  1. Carnival—Louisiana—New Orleans—Juvenile literature. 2. Carnival—Juvenile literature. 3. New Orleans (La.)—Social life and customs—Juvenile literature. I. Bryan-Hunt, Jan, ill. II. Title. III. Series.
  GT4211.N4H45 2006
  394.25—dc22   2005025685

TABLE OF CONTENTS

CHAPTER ONE

LET THE GOOD TIMES ROLL!

Everyone's wearing costumes. They're dancing in the streets. Parades with giant floats go by. And bead necklaces fly through the air. It's Mardi Gras (MAR-dee GRAH)!

Mardi Gras is a crazy, colorful carnival. The only rule is to have fun! Would you like to learn the Mardi Gras **motto**? Just say, *"Laissez les bon temps roulez"*! (LESS-ay leh bohn tohn roo-LAY) That's French. It means "Let the good times roll!"

Mardi Gras is a celebration filled with bright colors and exciting costumes!

CHAPTER TWO

FAT TUESDAY

Mardi Gras is a French name. It means "fat Tuesday"! That's the day before Ash Wednesday. In Christian tradition, Ash Wednesday is the first day of Lent.

Lent is the season before Easter. It's a time to think and pray. People think of things they do too much. They try to give up some things. That often means eating less. That's how Fat Tuesday got its name. It's the last chance to eat a lot!

Are you hungry? Fat Tuesday is a chance to enjoy your favorite foods.

CARNIVAL

Mardi Gras season is called Carnival. The word carnival *comes from two Latin words. They are* carnem *(meat) and* levare *(to remove). So* carnival *means "removing meat." Not eating meat was a common practice during Lent.*

CHAPTER THREE

A FRENCH CARNIVAL

When is Mardi Gras? Usually it takes place in February. But the fun begins on January 6. That's the start of Carnival season.

The excitement of the Carnival season begins in January.

TWELFTH NIGHT

January 6 is called Twelfth Night. It's the twelfth day after Christmas. Twelfth Night is another name for the Christian Feast of the Epiphany. It's said to be the day the Three Wise Men visited the infant Jesus.

The merrymaking lasts for weeks! There are parties, parades, and costume **balls.** It all leads up to the last big day. That's Fat Tuesday— which is Mardi Gras!

Mardi Gras is a French festival. How did it come to the United States? French settlers brought it.

Many French people settled in Louisiana. They arrived in the late 1600s and the 1700s. They kept up their Mardi Gras traditions in their new home. Where is the biggest Mardi Gras festival today? In New Orleans, Louisiana!

Carnival merrymaking includes music, parties, parades, and balls.

CHAPTER FOUR

THE KREWES OF NEW ORLEANS

Many Mardi Gras traditions got their start in New Orleans. One is the system of krewes (CREWS). A krewe is a Carnival club. New Orleans has dozens of krewes today.

Each krewe picks a Mardi Gras theme. It could be a nursery rhyme. It might be a legend. Or it may be a famous person or a faraway place. All the krewe's Carnival activities and decorations follow that theme.

Each krewe elects a king or queen. Some krewes also hold a masked ball. Everyone comes in costume, and many people wear masks. All the

Mardi Gras krewes feature bright colors, creative decorating, and a king or queen.

*The first official krewe
held a Mardi Gras parade
in 1857. It was called
the Mystick Krewe of
Comus. (Comus was
the ancient Greek god of
merrymaking.) Many
other krewes sprang up
after that.*

costumes match the theme. Krewe members often act out a story around the theme. Next, the king or queen appears. Then people dance into the night!

The dancing begins at a Mardi Gras ball when the king or queen appears.

CHAPTER FIVE

"THROW ME
SOMETHING, MISTER!"

What part of Mardi Gras is the most fun of all? The parades! Each krewe holds its own parade. Krewe members build huge floats, following their theme.

Each colorful float in a Mardi Gras parade follows a certain theme.

Mardi Gras

The floats are fantastic. They may look like giant animals or clowns. One float carries the king or queen. Bands march behind the floats. They play loud, lively tunes.

Thousands of people line the streets. They dance to the music. And they shout to the passing floats. It's a tradition to yell, "Throw me something, Mister!"

The krewes are ready. They throw necklaces of colored beads. They throw shiny doubloons, or metal coins. Some krewes throw candy or stuffed animals.

The parades last for twelve days. The last day is Fat Tuesday. On the stroke of midnight, the merrymaking ends. Lent has begun. It's time to settle down. But there's always next year!

Merrymakers enjoy Mardi Gras parades for twelve days!

The Krewe of Rex was organized in 1872. Rex is Latin for "king." The Krewe of Rex still exists today. Its parade is the biggest of all the Mardi Gras parades.

CHAPTER SIX

COSTUMES AND KING CAKES

Mardi Gras costumes can be very fancy! Many are purple, green, and gold. Those are the Mardi Gras colors.

People may dress as kings, queens, or clowns. Ruffles and glitter cover their colorful costumes. The masks glisten with shiny beads. Big, curly feathers stick out from the top or sides.

Jester costumes are favorites. A jester is a type of clown. Jesters used to do tricks for kings and queens. They wore crazy colors. And their hats had long, pointy tails with bells on each end.

Mardi Gras features people dressed as kings and jesters. Colorful, creative costumes are all part of the fun!

THE MARDI GRAS COLORS

Purple stands for justice.
Green stands for faith.
Gold stands for power.

King Cakes are a Mardi Gras tradition. A King Cake is shaped like a big donut. Purple, green, and gold sugar is sprinkled on top. Hidden inside is a tiny baby doll. What happens if you find the doll? You will have good luck. And you must buy the next King Cake!

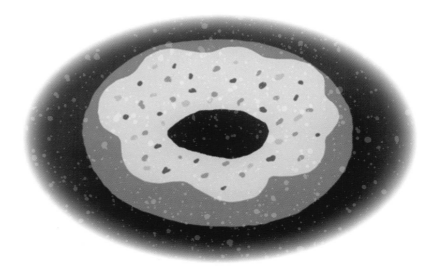

Want to find good luck in a taste treat? Try some King Cake!

THE THREE KINGS

King Cakes are based on the story of the Three Kings. The baby doll stands for the baby Jesus. Looking for the doll is like the kings' search for Jesus.

CHAPTER SEVEN

CARNIVAL AROUND THE WORLD

Many countries hold a Carnival before Lent. One is Brazil. Its biggest Carnival is in Rio de Janeiro. Dancers parade in glittery costumes with huge feathers. Giant floats go by. One might have a dragon spewing smoke. Another might look like a bird flapping its wings.

Germans celebrate Carnival, too. They call it "the foolish season." Some cities have Guilds of Fools. Each guild has its own style of costumes and masks. The masks often make fun of local leaders.

Venice, Italy, is famous for its masks. For Carnival, thousands of masked people parade in

the city square. Actors and acrobats put on shows
there, too. At last, fireworks light up the sky. Then
Carnival is over for another year.

*People all over the world celebrate Carnival
with different costumes and traditions.*

CHAPTER EIGHT

IF EVER I CEASE TO LOVE

This is a favorite Mardi Gras song. The song has many verses. They are very silly!

The title is repeated many times. Here, all the repeats are not shown. Then you can see the most silly lines!

If ever I cease to love,
If ever I cease to love,
May cows lay eggs and fish grow legs,
If ever I cease to love.

If ever I cease to love,
If ever I cease to love,
May little dogs wag their tails in front,
If ever I cease to love.

May all the seas turn into ink,
May I be made a king,
May conductors never knock down a cent,
May pigs be shot on the wing;
May cows lay eggs, may ducks give milk,
May an elephant turn to a dove,
May I never have to pay income tax
If ever I cease to love.

May sheep's heads grow on apple trees . . .
May a lion turn into a lamb . . .
May I have to live on pigeons' milk . . .
May the moon be turned into green cheese . . .
May I be stung to death with flies . . .
May all the streets be paved with gold . . .
May I be covered with diamond pins . . .
If ever I cease to love.

—From the 1870 musical show Blue Beard

Joining in the Spirit of Mardi Gras

- Make a Mardi Gras mask! Begin with a simple eye mask. Then paste your own decorations on it. You might use beads, feathers, and glitter.

- Make a Mardi Gras float. Begin with a shoebox. Then add the decorations. Try cloth flowers, sequins, buttons, ribbons, foil, or beads. Don't forget to add a throne for the king or queen!

- Make a Mardi Gras necklace. Begin with some dry ziti pasta. Paint the pasta pieces purple, green, and gold. Those are the Mardi Gras colors. String the pasta pieces on a long piece of yarn. Then let the good times roll!

Making King Cakes

Ingredients:

1 can refrigerated cinnamon rolls, with icing
   (Any brand of cinnamon rolls will do.)
¾ cup sugar
Blue, red, green, and yellow food coloring

Directions:

Separate the cinnamon rolls. Roll them out by hand so that they're long and thin, like hot dogs. Pinch the ends of each roll together to form an oval shape. Place the rolls on a cookie sheet, and bake according to the directions on the cinnamon-roll package.* While the rolls are cooking, divide the sugar into three parts of ¼ cup each. Use food coloring to dye one part green, one part gold (yellow), and one part purple. (You can combine the blue and red food coloring to create the color purple.) Once the rolls finish cooking, coat the tops with icing and sprinkle the colored sugar on each oval. Be sure to alternate the different colors. Use your sweet creation as a tasty way to celebrate Mardi Gras with friends!

Have an adult help you operate the oven.

Making a Mardi Gras Necklace

Colorful pasta beads in traditional Mardi Gras colors of purple, green, and gold are fun to make and wear.

What you need:

Uncooked dry pasta (Include a variety of shapes, but be sure each type of pasta has a hole through the middle.)

Paint or markers (Traditional Mardi Gras colors are purple, green, and gold.)

Glitter and glue, or glitter glue

1 18-inch-long piece of yarn or string

1 small piece of cardboard

Tape

Instructions:

1. Decorate your pasta shapes with paint, markers, and glitter. Be creative.
2. Let the paint, marker, and/or glue dry completely.
3. Tape one end of your yarn or string to the small piece of cardboard.
4. String as many pasta beads as you would like on your necklace.
5. Carefully remove the taped end of your string/yarn from the cardboard. Discard the tape.
6. Tie the two ends of your yarn or string together in a double knot.

Why not make necklaces for your family and friends?
Then you can all celebrate Mardi Gras in style!

Words to Know

balls *(BALLZ)* fancy dance parties where people dress up

cease *(SEES)* to stop doing something

guilds *(GILDZ)* groups of people who do the same type of work

justice *(JUSS-tiss)* fairness

legend *(LEH-jund)* an old story

motto *(MAH-toe)* a common saying

tradition *(truh-DISH-uhn)* a long-held custom

How to Learn More about Mardi Gras

At the Library

Couvillon, Alice, Elizabeth Moore, and Marilyn Carter Rougelot. *Mimi's First Mardi Gras.* Gretna, La: Pelican Publishing Company, 1992.

Shaik, Fatima, and Floyd Cooper (illustrator). *On Mardi Gras Day.* New York: Dial Books for Young Readers, 1999.

Vidrine, Beverly B., and Patrick Soper (illustrator). *A Mardi Gras Dictionary.* Gretna, La.: Pelican Publishing Company, 1997.

On the Web

Visit our home page for lots of links about Mardi Gras:
http://www.childsworld.com/links

NOTE TO PARENTS, TEACHERS, AND LIBRARIANS:
We routinely verify our Web links to make sure they're safe, active sites—so encourage your readers to check them out!

ABOUT THE AUTHOR

Ann Heinrichs lives in Chicago, Illinois. She has written more than two hundred books for children. She loves traveling to faraway places.

ABOUT THE ILLUSTRATOR

Jan Bryan-Hunt is a freelance illustrator living with her husband and two children in the Kansas City area.

Index